22.78

OCT 2004

**INDIAN TRAILS
PUBLIC LIBRARY DISTRICT**
WHEELING, ILLINOIS 60090
847-459-4100

DEMCO

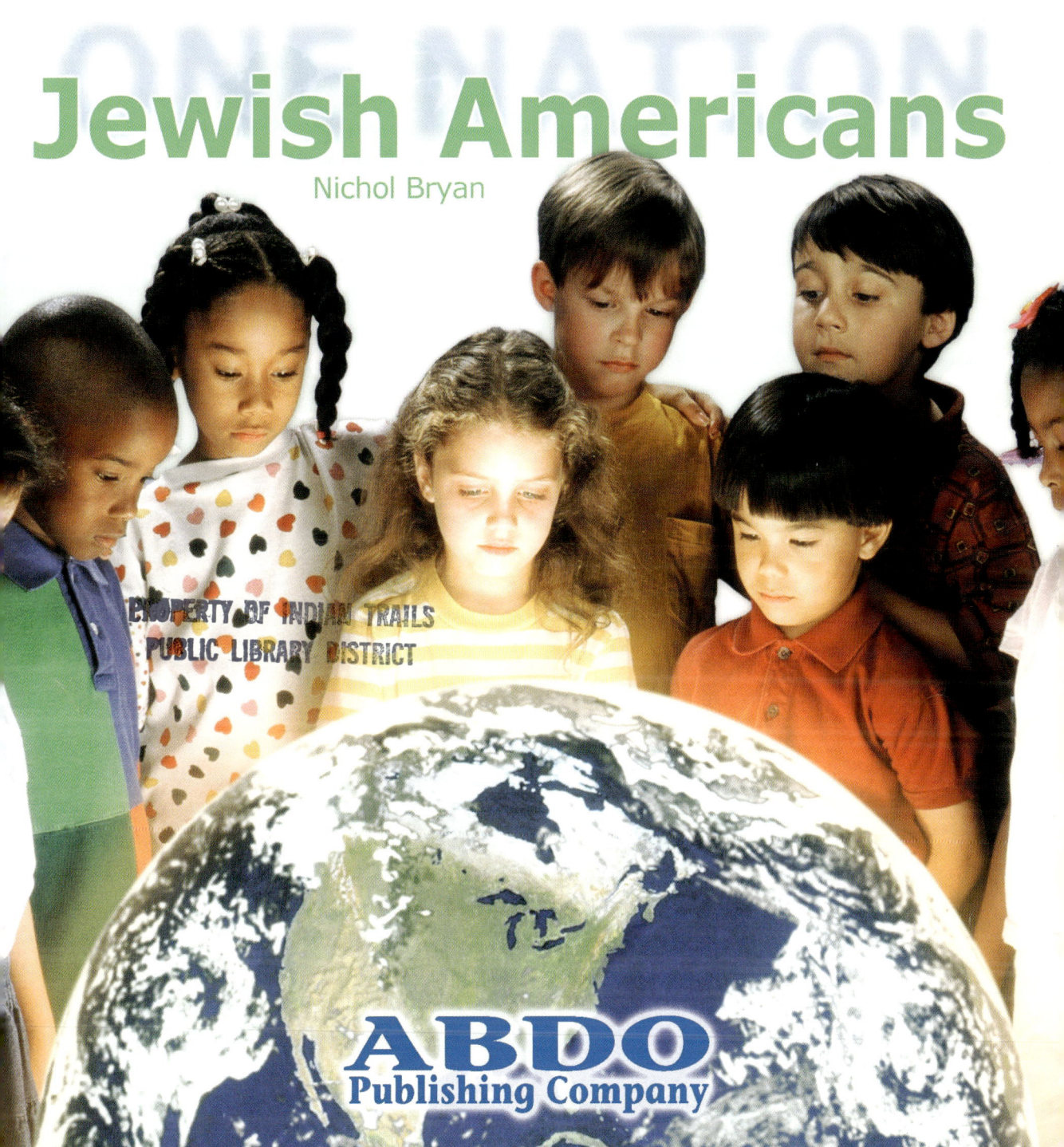

Jewish Americans

Nichol Bryan

ABDO Publishing Company

visit us at
www.abdopub.com

Published by ABDO Publishing Company, 4940 Viking Drive, Edina, Minnesota 55435. Copyright © 2004 by Abdo Consulting Group, Inc. International copyrights reserved in all countries. No part of this book may be reproduced in any form without written permission from the publisher.

Printed in the United States.

Cover Photo: Corbis
Interior Photos: AP/Wide World pp. 4, 24; Corbis pp. 1, 2-3, 6, 9, 10, 12, 13, 14, 16, 17, 19, 22, 23, 25, 27, 28, 29, 30-31; Getty Images pp. 23, 26, 28; Kayte Deioma pp. 5, 17, 20, 21

Editors: Kate A. Conley, Jennifer R. Krueger, Kristin Van Cleaf
Art Direction & Maps: Neil Klinepier

All of the U.S. population statistics in the One Nation series are taken from the 2000 Census.

Library of Congress Cataloging-in-Publication Data

Bryan, Nichol, 1958-
  Jewish Americans / Nichol Bryan.
    p. cm. -- (One nation)
  Summary: Provides an overview of the religion and culture of Jewish Americans and presents some information on the history of the Jewish people.
    Includes bibliographical references and index.
    ISBN 1-57765-986-4
  1. Jews--United States--History--Juvenile literature. 2. Jews--United States--Social life and customs--Juvenile literature. [1. Jews--United States. 2. Immigrants. 3. Refugees.] I. Title.

E184.35.B78 2003
973'.04924--dc21

2002043628

Contents

Jewish Americans 4
A People Apart 6
In America 12
Becoming a Citizen 18
Being Jewish 20
Part of America 26
Glossary 30
Saying It 31
Web Sites 31
Index 32

Jewish Americans

The United States is a country of **immigrants** and their descendants. People from all over the world have come to America seeking new lives and new opportunities. Many also came for religious reasons, including Jewish immigrants.

In some ways, Jewish immigrants are different from other immigrants who came to America. Jews don't have one specific homeland. They come from countries such as Germany, Russia, Poland, Spain, and Syria. They are of many ethnic groups. For example, there are European Jews, African Jews, Arab Jews, and even Asian Jews.

A Jewish-American girl knits hats for people with cancer as a service project for her Bas Mitzvah.

To be Jewish is to be part of a **culture** that is thousands of years old. No matter where they come from, what they look like, or how they worship, Jews all honor that same culture. It is part of what sets them apart as a people.

Jewish-American girls gather after their synagogue's evening Rosh Hashanah celebration.

A People Apart

The Jewish people trace their history back to Abraham. The **Hebrew Bible** tells the story of how Abraham settled in Canaan, an area now known as Palestine. Abraham's descendants were called the Israelites. For many years, the Israelites lived in Canaan. When a **famine** struck, they were invited to live in Egypt.

Many years later, an Egyptian pharaoh enslaved the Israelites. They worked in slavery until the 1200s B.C., when the prophet Moses led them out of Egypt. This period is known as the Exodus. The Israelites then wandered in the desert for 40 years.

Eventually, the Israelites returned to the land of Canaan. They formed a kingdom called Israel. The kingdom later split into two parts. The people called their southern kingdom Judah, with Jerusalem as its capital. From the name Judah, they became known as Jews.

Moses is one of the most important prophets in Judaism.

Around 722 B.C., the northern kingdom was conquered and destroyed. Its people were scattered, and they disappeared. Then in about 587 B.C., the Babylonians conquered Judah and destroyed the Temple of Jerusalem. The Jews were exiled to Babylon. This began what is called the Diaspora, or dispersion. Since then, the Jewish people have been scattered throughout the world.

The Kingdom of Israel in About 1000 B.C.

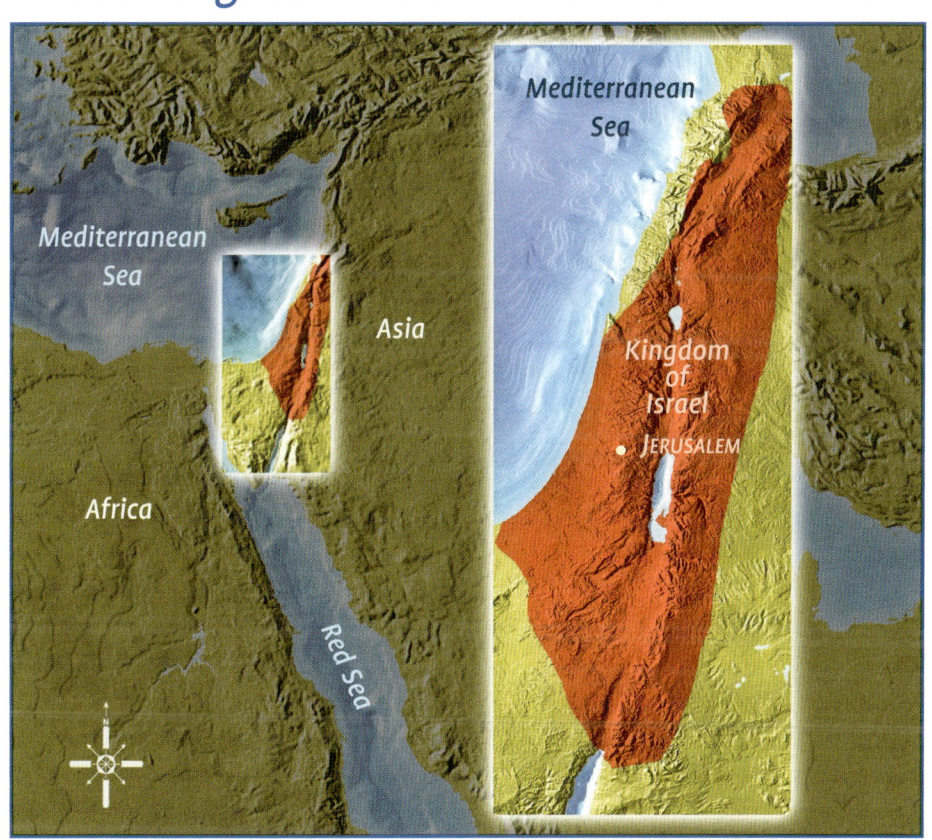

In 539 B.C., King Cyrus of Persia gained control of Judah and allowed the Jews to return. Some returned to rebuild the Temple of Jerusalem. The Jewish kingdom was later conquered by the Greeks and then the Romans. Around A.D. 70, the Romans destroyed the Temple of Jerusalem, driving out the Jews.

The Jews traveled around the world looking for a home. They moved to places such as Europe and northern Africa. In most places, Jews lived in communities separate from those around them. They believed it was the best way to preserve their **culture** and faith.

Even after Jews found places to settle, life was difficult. Jews were often considered outsiders. Some Christians distrusted Jews because they would not accept Christianity. And, rumors and stereotypes developed from lack of knowledge and understanding.

These factors sometimes led to **prejudice** and hatred. The **Crusades** that began in 1096 led to violent **anti-Semitism**. Jews were expelled from areas such as England and France. Fear even caused people to blame Jews for the **Black Death** of the mid-1300s.

In Spain in the 1400s, many Jews were forced to become Christians. But, many who converted practiced their Jewish faith secretly. In the late 1400s, the **Spanish Inquisition** persecuted these people. Eventually, all Jews were forced to leave Spain. Many of these Jews eventually came to the United States.

The Western Wall in Jerusalem is one of the holiest Jewish sites. It is all that remains of the Second Temple, destroyed by the Romans in A.D. 70.

The modern Israeli flag displays the Star of David, a traditional Jewish symbol.

In some lands, Jewish people were required to live in special areas called ghettos. Sometimes they even had to wear badges that identified them as Jewish. In the 1800s, **pogroms** in Russia destroyed many Jewish communities. This led to large-scale migration to the United States.

Then in 1933, Adolf Hitler and the Nazis came to power in Germany. They created laws limiting the rights of Jewish people, and they spread **prejudice** and hatred. Some Jews escaped to countries such as the United States. The less fortunate were sent to **concentration camps**. Before the end of World War II, the Nazis had killed 6 million Jews. This mass murder became known as the Holocaust.

After World War II, Jews called Zionists created a new Jewish homeland in Palestine. They called their country Israel. Since then, millions of Jews have moved there. But, many more remain in the lands to which they have scattered. One of those places is the United States.

Major Waves of Jewish Migration to the United States

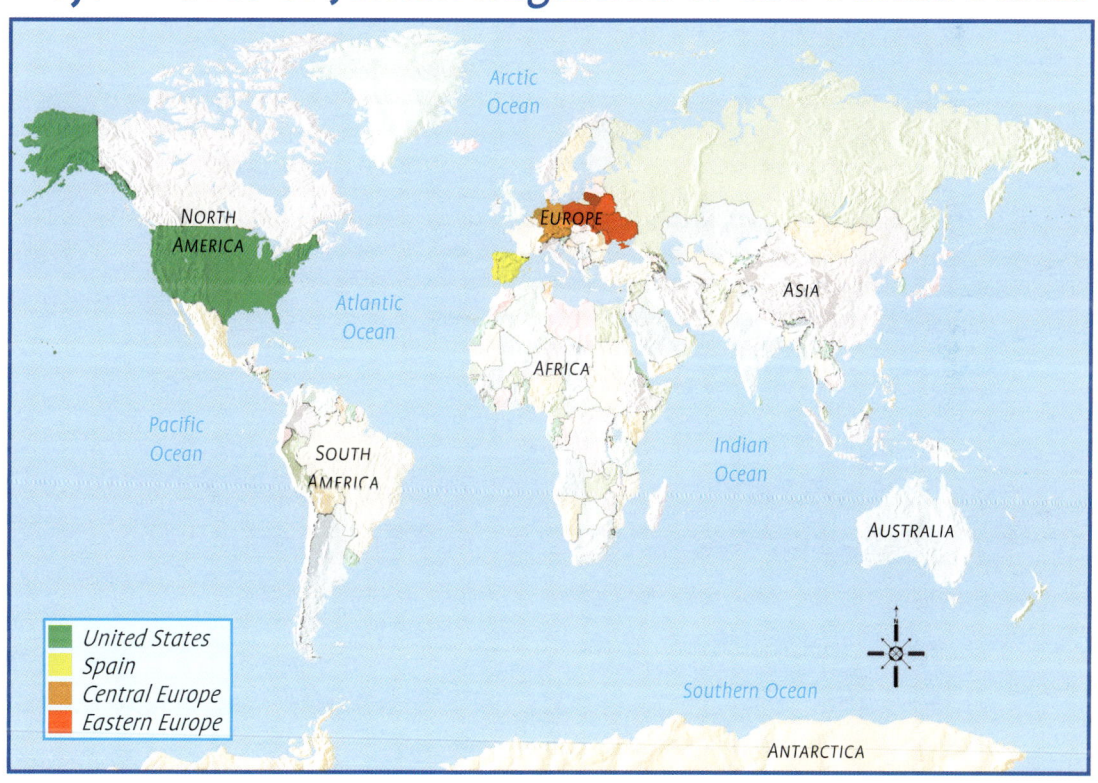

In America

The first group of Jewish people to land in North America arrived in 1654. More followed this first group, settling along the East Coast. By 1776, there were around 2,500 Jews living in America.

The first large wave of Jewish **immigrants** arrived in America in the mid-1800s. They had left Germany and central Europe to escape political and **economic** troubles. Many of the German Jews began their life in America as peddlers. As the United States grew, some settled in the western territories. Eventually, many of these Jewish immigrants became successful bankers and merchants.

Jewish immigrants found America to be a land of opportunity. At times they faced **anti-Semitism** and stereotypes. But overall, they were accepted into society. Many became successful business leaders and blended into everyday American life.

A Russian Jewish immigrant arrives at Ellis Island in 1900.

Orthodox Jews shop at a market in New York's Lower East Side in 1926.

The largest wave of Jewish **immigrants** came between 1881 and 1924. During those years, nearly 2.5 million Jews flocked to the United States. They came to escape Russian **pogroms** and the crushing poverty found in eastern Europe. Once in the United States, most of them took low-paying jobs as petty traders and factory workers.

These new Jewish immigrants had come from small, enclosed communities called shtetlach. In America, they settled in crowded neighborhoods in New York's Lower East Side. Or, they moved to cities such as Chicago, Boston, and Philadelphia. In these places they set up tightly knit communities. They built synagogues and spoke their own language, **Yiddish**. They even started Yiddish newspapers and theaters.

However, these new eastern European communities stood out. It was this wave of **immigrants** that began the first significant **anti-Semitism** in the United States. Clubs and resorts began excluding Jews. Old stereotypes began to influence Americans' views of their Jewish neighbors.

Two Jewish boys living in Minnesota in 1908

By World War I, some colleges were limiting the number of Jewish students they would accept. Jews also had trouble finding jobs in large businesses or in fields such as journalism. In 1924, the Immigration Restriction Act set a limit that slowed migration to the United States. However, much of the worst **prejudice** against Jews

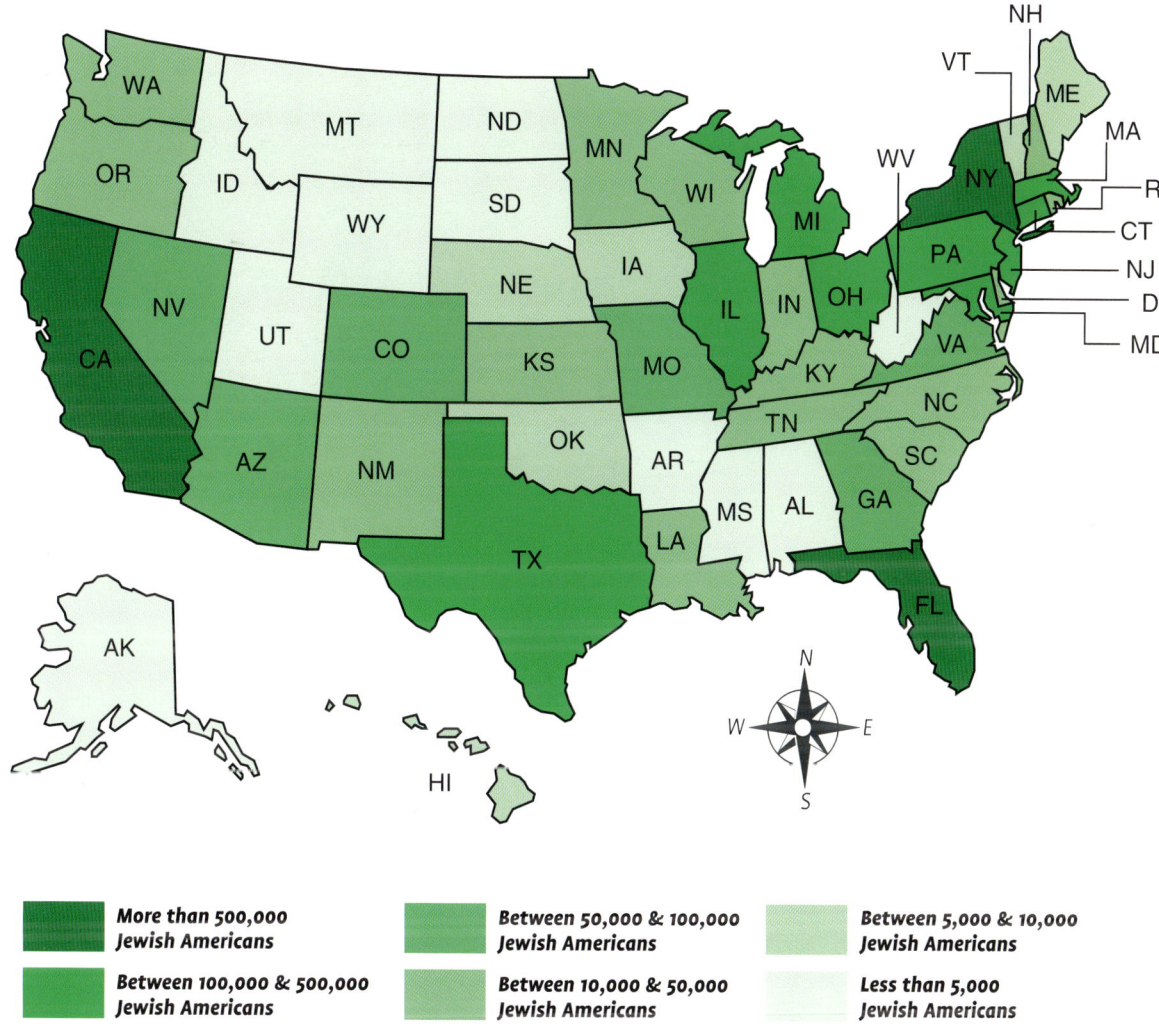

In the 1930s, whole families fled Europe to escape the Nazis.

occurred in the 1930s. During that time, many Jews were accused of being **communists**. This suspicion developed because so many Jewish Americans had Russian **heritage**.

Many Jews had feared that blending into U.S. society would mean losing their Jewish identity. But, some believed that the best way to cope with **anti-Semitism** was to learn English and adopt more American ways. American-born Jews set up societies, schools, and health-care centers to support new arrivals and help them adjust to American society.

A Jewish-American Brownie Girl Scout

Immigration laws remained strict throughout the 1930s and 1940s. During these years, more Jews came to America to escape the Holocaust. Many were leading scientists, artists, writers, and educators. More came after the end of World War II.

The Holocaust showed many Americans the evil that **anti-Semitism** could cause. Jews still sometimes faced **prejudice** after World War II. However, social conditions improved overall. More Jewish Americans became known in business, entertainment, academics, law, and medicine.

Today, more than 5 million Americans are Jewish. Some have blended into American society. Others live in communities that continue to be tightly knit groups. While fewer Jewish immigrants come to the United States today, they still arrive from all over the world to find a freer, richer life.

Hasidic Jewish Americans follow strict interpretations of the Torah. These two wear the hair in front of their ears long as part of their beliefs.

Becoming a Citizen

Jews and other **immigrants** who come to the United States take the same path to citizenship. Immigrants become citizens in a process called naturalization. A government agency called the Immigration and Naturalization Service (INS) oversees this process.

The Path to Citizenship

Applying for Citizenship

The first step in becoming a citizen is filling out a form. It is called the Application for Naturalization. On the application, immigrants provide information about their past. Immigrants send the application to the INS.

Providing Information

Besides the application, immigrants must provide the INS with other items. They may include documents such as marriage licenses or old tax returns. Immigrants must also provide photographs and fingerprints. They are used for identification. The fingerprints are also used to check whether immigrants have committed crimes in the past.

The Interview

Next, an INS officer interviews each immigrant to discuss his or her application and background. In addition, the INS officer tests the immigrant's ability to speak, read, and write in English. The officer also tests the immigrant's knowledge of American civics.

The Oath

Immigrants approved for citizenship must take the Oath of Allegiance. Once immigrants take this oath, they are citizens. During the oath, immigrants promise to renounce loyalty to their native country, to support the U.S. Constitution, and to serve and defend the United States when needed.

Sample Questions from the Civics Test

How many stars are there on our flag?

What is the capital of the state you live in?

Why did the pilgrims come to America?

How many senators are there in Congress?

Who said, "Give me liberty or give me death"?

What are the first 10 amendments to the Constitution called?

In what month do we vote for the president?

Why Become a Citizen?

Why would an immigrant want to become a U.S. citizen? There are many reasons. Perhaps the biggest reason is that the U.S. Constitution grants many rights to its citizens. One of the most important is the right to vote.

Being Jewish

What makes a person Jewish? You might say that Jews share the same religion. But, religious Jews worship in very different ways. Some are strict Orthodox or even Hasidic Jews. Other Jewish people may be Reform or Conservative. However, anyone whose mother is Jewish is also considered Jewish.

Some Jewish people wear small caps called yarmulkes as a sign of their faith.

Jews were among the first people to believe in only one God. Jews believe that God has a special agreement with the Jewish people, called a covenant. They believe God will take care of them as long as they follow his laws.

The Jewish holy book is called the Torah. The Torah contains many rules on how a Jew should live. From these laws, Jews have developed many **customs** and traditions.

Jewish life is guided by religious leaders called rabbis. They teach about the Torah and advise people on their problems. Jews gather in synagogues to pray and hear readings from the Torah.

Being Jewish

Prayer shawls, or talliths, were traditionally only worn by men. Today, many Jewish-American women wear them as well.

Family

The family is the center of life for most Jewish Americans. Parents take care to pass on their faith to their children. Jewish boys and girls each receive a Hebrew name soon after they are born.

A Jewish boy is named in a ritual called the Brith Milah. It is held on the eighth day after the boy's birth. A Jewish girl is usually named in a simpler ceremony on the first Sabbath after her birth. Recently, some Jewish families have begun holding a more formal ceremony for girls, too. Both ceremonies involve prayers and celebration for the newborn child.

Another important day in a Jewish boy's life is when he has his Bar Mitzvah. This is when he reaches the age of 13 and officially takes on the personal and religious responsibilities of an adult. Today, many Jewish girls celebrate turning 12 in a similar ceremony called a Bas Mitzvah.

A Jewish girl reads from the Torah for her Bas Mitzvah.

Food

Dietary laws are part of the Jewish faith. For instance, the Torah forbids Jews from eating pork or shellfish. They also should not consume meat and milk at the same time. And, the meat they do eat should be prepared in a special way. Such food is called kosher.

A plate of traditional food for a Seder

Some foods are special and eaten during rituals and holy days. For example, challah is a braided bread eaten on the Sabbath and some holidays. Matzo is a flat, crispy bread eaten during Passover.

The bread the Israelites baked before fleeing Egypt didn't have time to rise. Eating matzo at Passover is a reminder of this time.

A Language of Their Own

Jews came to America speaking all sorts of languages. However, Hebrew has been the Jewish language throughout history. Hebrew is the ancient language of the Torah. Jews learn Hebrew in order to read and study the Torah. Even today, Jewish prayers are said in Hebrew.

Books written in Yiddish

Many Jewish **immigrants** who arrived from eastern Europe also spoke **Yiddish**. In America, they clung to this language as part of their tradition. But, as these immigrants and their children mixed with American society, Yiddish faded from everyday life. Today, this language is mainly spoken in strictly traditional communities.

Holy Days

Jewish Americans observe a number of special days as part of their faith. One of the most important of these days is the Sabbath. It starts every Friday at sundown and ends at sundown on Saturday. On the Sabbath, Jewish people say a blessing over a special meal and rest from the week's work.

Being Jewish

In addition to the Sabbath, Jews have other special days. The most sacred days are Rosh Hashanah and Yom Kippur, which are called the High Holy Days. Jews also have three major festivals called Shabuoth, Sukkoth, and Passover.

Passover commemorates the Exodus. Jewish Americans observe this holiday for eight days. On the first and second nights, Jewish-American families eat a special meal called a Seder. The foods served are symbolic of the Exodus. They include matzo, lamb, bitter herbs, and salt water.

Some other special Jewish holidays are Purim and Hanukkah. On Purim, Jews celebrate how Queen Esther saved Persian Jews from being killed by her prime minister, Haman. Hanukkah celebrates the miracle that occurred after the Jews retook the Temple of Jerusalem from the Syrians. For eight nights, Jewish families light candles on a special nine-branched stand called a menorah.

Hanukkah dinner after lighting the menorah

Part of America

Senator Joseph Lieberman and his wife, Hadassah

Jewish Americans have influenced many parts of American society. One way they have done this is by getting involved in the government. For example, Arthur Goldberg was a Supreme Court justice and a U.S. ambassador to the United Nations. In 2000, Senator Joseph Lieberman was the first Jewish American nominated for vice president of the United States.

Jewish Americans have also contributed to science. The best-known Jewish scientist was physicist Albert Einstein. His theories on time and space earned him a Nobel Prize. This German-born scientist came to America in 1933 to escape the Nazis. Although Einstein didn't practice his faith, he was a strong supporter of Israel.

In medicine, Jewish-American nurse Lillian D. Wald was a pioneer in public health. Wald saw the need for public health care in New York's Lower East Side. She set up a facility there to provide for the poor families of the area. Later, Wald helped to get nurses in public schools. She also organized classes on home health care, cooking, and sewing.

Many popular comedians also share a Jewish **heritage**. The Marx Brothers were a team of four Jewish Americans. They made a string of hit stage shows and movies in the 1920s, 1930s, and 1940s that are still enjoyed today. Other Jewish-American comedians include Jack Benny, Jerry Seinfeld, and Adam Sandler.

The Marx Brothers, from the left: Harpo, Groucho, Zeppo, and Chico Marx

Barbra Streisand

Jewish-American singers have been popular since the days of Al Jolson. He sang in the first talking movie, *The Jazz Singer*, in 1927. Perhaps the most famous Jewish-American singer is Barbra Streisand. Since the 1960s, she has released a number of best-selling albums. She has also starred in Broadway shows and movies. She even directed a movie called *Yentl*. It is about a Jewish girl who disguises herself as a boy in order to go to college.

Irving Berlin and George Gershwin are also important in American music. They were two of the twentieth century's greatest composers of popular songs. Bandleader Benny Goodman made jazz a popular form of music in the 1930s and 1940s. Jewish-American classical composer Aaron Copland wrote *Rodeo* and *Appalachian Spring*. They are two classic pieces of American music.

Irving Berlin's "White Christmas" is one of the most popular songs ever recorded.

The Jewish-American poet Emma Lazarus has also contributed to the United States. She has a special place not only in the history of Jewish **immigrants**, but also in the history of all those who came looking for a better life in America. One of her poems, "The New Colossus," is written on the pedestal of the Statue of Liberty. "Give me your tired, your poor, your huddled masses yearning to breathe free," she wrote.

It's hard to imagine what American life would be like without the contributions of Jewish Americans. These people have managed to keep many of their own traditions, while still blending into American society. At the same time, they have made all Americans richer. They have changed what it means to be an American.

Emma Lazarus wrote many essays in defense of persecuted Jews in the late 1800s.

Glossary

anti-Semitism - hostility or discrimination toward the Jewish people.
Black Death - a deadly disease that spread throughout Europe between 1347 and 1352.
communism - a social and economic system in which everything is owned by the government and is distributed to the people as needed.
concentration camp - a camp where political enemies and prisoners of war are held.
Crusades - a series of conflicts between European Christians and Muslims in Palestine. The Crusades resulted in strong feelings against anyone not Christian.
culture - the customs, arts, and tools of a nation or people at a certain time.
customs - the habits of a group that are passed on through generations.
economy - the way a nation uses its money, goods, and natural resources.
famine - a severe scarcity of food.
Hebrew Bible - the Jewish Bible, including most of the Old Testament. It includes the books of Moses (or Torah), the books of the prophets, and books such as Psalms.
heritage - the handing down of something from one generation to the next.
immigration - entry into another country to live. People who immigrate are called immigrants.
pogrom - the organized persecution or massacre of a minority group.
prejudice - hatred of a particular group based on factors such as race or religion.
Spanish Inquisition - a Catholic court in the 1400s designed to capture and punish former Jews and Muslims who didn't follow official Church beliefs and practices.
Yiddish - a language spoken by Jews of European descent. Yiddish developed in Jewish communities in Europe and was spoken for hundreds of years.

Saying It

Bas Mitzvah - bahs-MIHTS-vuh
Brith Milah - BRIHT mee-LAH
George Gershwin - JAWRJ GUHRSH-wuhn
Hasidic - ha-SIH-dihk
Israelite - IHZ-ruh-lite
Joseph Lieberman - JOH-zuhf LEEB-uhr-muhn
Judah - JOO-duh
rabbi - RA-by
Seder - SAY-duhr
Shabuoth - shuh-VOO-oht
shtetlach - SHTEHT-lahkh
Sukkoth - SUH-kuhs
synagogue - SIH-nuh-gahg
yarmulke - YAH-muh-kuh

Web Sites

To learn more about Jewish Americans, visit ABDO Publishing Company on the World Wide Web at **www.abdopub.com**. Web sites about Jewish Americans are featured on our Book Links page. These links are routinely monitored and updated to provide the most current information available.

Index

A
Abraham 6
Africa 8
anti-Semitism 8, 10, 12, 14, 16, 17

B
Babylon 7
Benny, Jack 27
Berlin, Irving 28
Boston, Massachusetts 14

C
Canaan 6
Chicago, Illinois 14
citizenship 18
Copland, Aaron 28
Cyrus (king of Persia) 8

D
Diaspora 7

E
Egypt 6
Einstein, Albert 26
England 8
Europe 8, 12, 13, 24
Exodus 6, 25

F
family 22, 25, 27
food 23, 25
France 8

G
Germany 4, 10, 12, 26
Gershwin, George 28
Goldberg, Arthur 26
Goodman, Benny 28

H
history 6, 7, 8, 10, 11, 12, 13, 14, 16, 17, 24
Hitler, Adolf 10
Holocaust 10, 17
holy days 22, 23, 24, 25

I
immigration 4, 10, 12, 13, 14, 17, 18, 24, 26, 29
Immigration and Naturalization Service 18
Israel 6, 11, 26
Israelites 6

J
Jerusalem 6, 7, 8, 25
Jerusalem, Temple of 7, 8, 25
Jolson, Al 28
Judah 6, 7, 8

L
language 14, 16, 24
Lazarus, Emma 29

Lieberman, Joseph 26
Lower East Side 13, 27

M
Marx Brothers 27
Moses 6

N
New York, New York 13, 27
North America 12

P
Palestine 6, 11
Philadelphia, Pennsylvania 14
pogroms 10, 13
Poland 4

R
religion 4, 8, 20, 22, 23, 24, 25
Russia 4, 10

S
Sandler, Adam 27
Seinfeld, Jerry 27
Spain 4, 8
Streisand, Barbra 28
Syria 4

W
Wald, Lillian D. 27
World War I 14
World War II 10, 11, 17

3 1125 00565 7414